DREAM DECODER

What are your Dreams Telling You!

Termina

Copyright © 2017 by Termina

All rights reserved. No part of this book may be reproduced, scanned, or distributed in any printed or electronic form without permission.

Perpelflame Independent Media Publishing P.I.M.P Publications 2018. Perpelflame Independent Media Publishing P.I.M.P Publications does not participate in, endorse, or have any authority or responsibility concerning private business arrangements between our authors and the public.

This book is designed to provide information and inspiration to readers. It is sold with the understanding that the author is not engaged to render any type of psychological, legal, or any other kind of professional advice. The content of each article is the sole expression and opinion of its author. No warranties or guarantees are expressed or implied by the author's choice to include any of the content in this volume. The author shall have no liability or responsibility to any person or entity regarding physical, psychological, emotional, financial, commercial damages, special, incidental, or consequential by the information contained in this book.

TABLE OF CONTENTS

Introduction

Did We Always Dream?

Sigmund Freud on Dreams

Carl Jung on Dreams

Edgar Cayce on Dreams

Types of Dreams

Why Do We Dream?

Why Remember Your Dreams?

How to Remember Your Dreams

Interpreting Your Dreams

Most Common Dream Images

Teeth Falling Out

Flying

Being Caught In A Tornado

Being Naked

Being Chased

Falling

Taking an Exam or Test

Dream Symbols

Animals

People

Babies/Pregnancy

Sex

- Snakes
- Fire
- Trains
- Driving
- Ex-Partners
- Cheating
- School
- A House
- Colours
- Death
- Love/Lust
- Aliens
- Angels
- Children
- Dead People
- Accidents
- Nightmares
- Disturbing Dreams
- Conclusion

INTRODUCTION

"A dream may be of a physical, mental, or spiritual nature and may deal with all manner of psychic manifestations. These include telepathy, clairvoyance, prophetic visions, out of body traveling, remembrance of past lives, communication with beings in other realms including deceased friends and relatives, spirit guides, angels, Christ, and even the voice of God. Dreams can also give invaluable information on the status of the body."

– Edgar Cayce

"I had a dream last night, or, I had the **strangest dream** last night!"

How many times have you said these similar words, even heard it from others?

People are fascinated, even frightened with the moving images that play out during sleep. Some believe that dreams can predict the future. Others say that dreams depict real life. Still others believe that dreams are a manifestation of what we want to be or a message to be considered.

Interpreting dreams has evolved over the years to what some consider an art form. We spend one-third of our lives sleeping. In the average lifetime, six years is spent dreaming. That's more than 2,100 days spent in a different world! Every night, we dream on an average of one to two hours and usually have 4-7 dreams per night.

Sleep Cycle and Dreaming

When preparing to sleep we move from brain patterns known as alpha and beta waves, our awake phase. Sleep begins, and we move into another pattern named, theta waves (restorative sleep phase). As we go deeper into sleep, we then move into brain patterns known as delta waves. Delta waves are the slowest and highest volume brain waves. Delta sleep is our deepest sleep where the stage of REM (rapid eye movement) sleep exists. The brain wave patterns in this stage, show characteristics similar to alpha and beta waves (our waking phases), and this is the juncture of sleep associated with dreaming. It is due to the similar characteristics of alpha and beta waves that many of our dreams feel very real.

Consider some of these facts about dreams and dreaming:

- Everybody dreams. EVERYBODY! Simply because you do not remember your dream does not mean that you did not dream. According to a group of sleep researchers in France, they state. "All people dream when they sleep, even people who think they don't."

- Dreams are indispensable. A lack of dream activity can mean protein deficiency or a personality disorder. They emerge during the deepest levels of relaxation and restorative, healing sleep. This deep sleep has also been found to aid in unconscious bodily functions such as regulating heart beat and digestion. If there is lack in delta wave activity, people may experience learning disabilities.

- Men tend to dream more about other men, while women dream equally about men and women.

- People who are giving up smoking have longer and more intense dreams.

- Toddlers do not dream about themselves. They do not appear in their own dreams until the age of 3 or 4.

- If you are snoring, then you cannot be dreaming. Snoring is the vibration of respiratory functions and the result of obstructed air movement during breathing while sleeping. The delta wave activity of dreams requires relaxation of respiratory functions.

- Blind people do dream. Whether visual images will appear in their dream depends on whether they were blind at birth or became blind later in life. But vision is not the only sense that constitutes a dream. Sounds, tactility, and smell become hypersensitive for the blind and their dreams are based on these senses.

The dream world is fascinating, full of speculation, hope, and sometimes even fear. We can wake up from a good dream feeling refreshed and hopeful. On the other hand, we can wake up from a bad dream feeling tense, apprehensive and even concerned.

Ever since *"Interpretation of Dreams"* by Sigmund Freud, was published, there has been recognition of the importance of dreams.

Freud emphasised, *"the importance of the unconscious mind, with respect to dream interpretation and his primary theory is that the unconscious mind governs behaviour to a greater degree than people suspect, and the goal of psychoanalysis is to make the unconscious conscious."*

But even before Freud there were dream interpretations. People had superstitious notions about dreams - for example, something is going to happen because it showed up in a dream."

This is a common misconception. Regardless of what some people might say, if you dream you are falling and don't wake up before you hit the ground in your dream, you will not die. If you dream that someone close to you dies, that's not an omen to warn you of their death. Dreams are not literal and often they deliver messages opposite to the moving images – for example, death can depict change or long life.

What dreams can do is provide a sense of insight into ourselves. They can help us with situations we're unsure about. They can guide us in a certain direction when faced with uncertainty. They can simply give us an overall good feeling as we dream of something pleasant.

The dream state is a Divine guide and experimental playground which gives you a chance to explore and express emotions without the usual inhibitions you may display in your waking life. Dreams provide an avenue of expression for the part of yourself that knows both your history and your potential as a spiritual being.

They are another way the universe, or our Divine provides guidance about relationships, careers, and health problems. Through dreams you may find answers to your spiritual questions and even receive encouragement to some challenge in your life. While some dreams may allow you to release bottled emotions from your day's activities, others can lead to profound insights in a psychological or spiritual way.

Acquiring the ability to interpret your dreams is a powerful tool. In analysing dreams, you can learn about your deep secrets and hidden feelings. No one is a better expert at interpreting your dreams than yourself.

In the following pages of this book, we will look at dreams and dreaming as a science as well as the various meanings that dream content can have. This is not meant to be a definitive guide to dreams. It is simply a starting point for you to look at what "moving pictures" your sub-conscious is creating and guiding you for, and how you can apply it your life to affect change if needed.

Remember that a dream unifies the body, mind, and spirit. It provides you with insight into yourself and a means for self-exploration. In understanding your dreams, you will have a better understanding and discovery of your true self, your Divine self. So explore, enjoy, and discover what guidance is in your dreams!

DID WE ALWAYS DREAM?

That may seem like a silly question but think about early man. Have people always dreamt even when the world around them was quite simple and mundane? The answer is yes. While we cannot have definitive proof of prehistoric man, we can know that back in Ancient Rome that striking and significant dreams were submitted to the Senate for analysis and interpretation.

What did man do with these odd images that appeared during their sleep? Well, they did what we do today – they interpreted them!

Dream interpretations date back to 3000-4000 B.C. where they were documented on clay tablets. For as long as we have been able to communicate our dreams, we have been fascinated with them and strive to understand them.

People in primal societies were unable to distinguish between the dream world and reality. They not only saw the dream world as an extension of reality, but that the dream realm was a more powerful world, raising the question of where are we when we are in a dream state.

Back in the Greek and Roman era, dreams were often seen in a religious context and messages from the gods. Temples, called Asclepieions were built around the power of dreams. It was believed that sick people who slept in these temples would be sent cures through their dreams.

In Egypt, priests also acted as dream interpreters. The Egyptians recorded their dreams in hieroglyphics. People with particular vivid and significant dreams were believed to be blessed and were considered special. People who had the power to interpret dreams were looked up to and seen as divinely gifted. In the bible, there are over seven hundred mentions of dreams. Tracing back to these ancient cultures, people had always had an inclination to interpret dreams

Dreams were also seen as prophetic and an omen from outside spirits. People often looked to their dreams for signs of warning, advice from a deity, from the dead or even the works of a demon. Sometimes they look to their dreams for what to do or what course of action to take.

Dreams often dictated the actions of political and military leaders. In fact, in the Green and Roman era, dream interpreters even accompanied military leaders into battle to help. Some interpreters aided the medicine men in a diagnosis.

Dreams offered a vital clue for healers in finding what was wrong with the dreamer.

Dreaming can be seen as an actual place that your spirit and soul leaves every night to go and visit. The Chinese believed that the soul leaves the body to go into this world. However, if they should be suddenly awakened, their soul may fail to return to the body. For this reason, some Chinese today, are wary of alarm clocks.

Some Native American tribes and Mexican civilizations share this same notion of a distinct dream dimension. They believed that their ancestors lived in their dreams and take on non-human forms like plants. They see that dreams as a way of visiting and having contact with their ancestors. Dreams also helped to point their mission or role in life.

During the Middle Ages, dreams were seen as evil and its images were temptations from the devil. In the vulnerable sleep state, the devil was believed to fill the mind of humans with poisonous thoughts. He did his dirty work though dreams attempting to mislead humans down a wrong path.

In the early 19th century, dreams were dismissed as stemming from anxiety, a household noise or even indigestion. Hence there was really no meaning to it. Later on in the 19th century, Sigmund Freud revived the importance of dreams and its significance and need for interpretation. He revolutionized the study of dreams.

Sigmund Freud on Dreams

Sigmund Freud actually called dreams the *"royal road to the unconscious,"* That statement will probably remain true in psychology forever. Freud's classic text, The Interpretation of Dreams, contains some of his finest work.

Freud believed every dream is a wish fulfilment, and he kept this theory to the end, even though he gave up his initial idea that all dreams have a sexual content.

For Freud, the concept of wish fulfilment didn't necessarily imply that a pleasure was sought, because a person could just as well have a wish to be punished. Nevertheless, this idea of a "secret" wish being masked by a dream remains central to classical Freudian psychoanalysis.

Freud said, *"Dreams are not comparable to the spontaneous sounds made by a musical instrument struck rather by some external force than by the hand of a performer; they are not meaningless, not absurd, they do not imply that one portion of our stockpile of ideas sleeps while another begins to awaken. They are a completely valid psychological phenomenon, specifically the fulfilment of wishes; they can be classified in the continuity of comprehensible waking mental states; they are constructed through highly complicated intellectual activity."*

It was not until Freud noticed how allowing his patients to freely associate ideas with whatever came to mind, that he really explored spontaneous abreaction. Freud himself suffered bouts of deep anxiety, and it was partly this that led him to explore the connection between association of ideas and dreams. In 1897 he wrote to his friend Wilhelm Fliess:

'No matter what I start with, I always find myself back again with the neuroses and the psychical apparatus. Inside me there is a seething ferment, and I am only waiting for the next surge forward. I have felt impelled to start writing about dreams, with which I feel on firm ground.'

This move toward dreams may have come about because in allowing his patients freedom to talk and explore the associations that arose - free association - Freud noticed that patients would often find a connection between the direction of their associations and a dream they had experienced. The more he allowed his patients to go in their own direction, the more frequently they mentioned their dreams. Also, talking about the dream often enabled the patient to discover a new and productive chain of associations and memories.

Freud began to take note of his own dreams and explore the associations they aroused. In doing so he was the first person to consciously and consistently explore a dream into its depths through uncovering and following obvious and hidden associations and emotions connected with the dream imagery and drama.

Obviously previous dream researchers had noticed how the dream image associated with personal concerns, but Freud broke through into seeing the connection with sexual feelings, with early childhood trauma, and with the subtleties of the human psyche. He did this to deal with his own neurosis, and he says of this period, 'I have been through some kind of neurotic experience, with odd states of mind not intelligible to consciousness, cloudy thoughts and veiled doubts, with barely here and there a ray of light.'

Using dreams for his self-analysis, Freud discovered that previously unremembered details from his childhood were recaptured along with feelings and states of mind which he had never met before.

He wrote of this period, *"Some sad secrets of life are being traced back to their first roots; the humble origins of much pride and precedence are being laid bare. I am now experiencing myself all the things that, as a third party, I have witnessed going on in my patients, days when I slink about depressed because I have understood nothing of the day's dreams, fantasies, or mood."*

Without this powerful and personal experience of working with his dreams, meeting emotions and fantasies welling up from the unconscious, Freud would not have so passionately believed in his theories regarding dreams and the unconscious.

Of course, like much of Freud's theories, he related dreams to sex. One of his basic views of dreams was that the purpose of dreams is to allow us to satisfy in fantasies the instinctual urges that society judges unacceptable such as sexual practices. This was partly the reason for the enormous opposition and criticism that he met.

During the period of his early life, only men were believed to have powerful sexual urges. When Freud showed that repressed but obvious sexual desires were equally at work in women this created a social uproar. Perhaps his second finding in regard to sexuality surprised even him. During his analysis of women patients, sexual advance or assault by the woman's father was often revealed.

Freud struggled with this, wondering whether the assault was memory of an actual event, or a psychic reproduction of it. He eventually came to the conclusion that hysterical and neurotic behaviour was often due to the trauma caused by an early sexual assault by the parent. Where there was no evidence of physical assault, then he saw the neurosis as due to sexual conflict or a trauma caused by some other event. This conflict was often manifested through dreams. This led to Freud being rejected by university colleagues, fellow doctors, and even by patients.

Another expert in the field of dreams and dream interpretation was Carl Jung.

Carl Jung on Dreams

Jung studied under the tutelage of Sigmund Freud. Their differing views on dreams and dream interpretations led to a permanent rift that led them to go their separate ways.

Like Freud, Jung believed in the existence of the unconscious. However, he didn't see the unconscious as animalistic, instinctual, and sexual; he saw it as more spiritual. Dreams were a way of communicating and acquainting ourselves with the unconscious. Dreams were not attempts to conceal our true feelings from the waking mind, but rather they were a window to our unconscious. They served to guide the waking self to achieve wholeness. Dreams offered a solution to a problem we are facing in our waking life.

Jung viewed the ego as one's sense of self and how we portray ourselves to the world. Part of Jung's theory was that all things can be viewed as paired opposites (i.e. good/evil, male/female, or love/hate). And thus, working in opposition to the ego, is the *"counter-ego"* or what he referred to as the shadow. The shadow represents rejected aspects of yourself that you do not wish to acknowledge. It is considered an aspect of yourself which is somewhat more primitive, uncultured, and awkward."

He said, "Dreams are the main source of all of our knowledge about symbolism." This means that the messages you receive from your dreams are expressed symbolically and must be interpreted to find their true meanings.

Jung says that rarely do the symbols in dreams have just one meaning. And when interpreting the messages in your dreams, he suggests going with your first hunch, relying on your intuitive abilities, before applying more rational methods of dream interpretation.

Perhaps one of the most fascinating dream theorists might be Edgar Cayce. Today, we would call him a psychic. When he was alive, he was a fascinating individual who, it appeared, could speak with the dead, make predictions about the future, and provide insight into areas where the normal person couldn't go.

Edgar Cayce on Dreams

Cayce was able to obtain virtually an unlimited amount of knowledge on an unlimited number of subjects. One of these subjects was dreams and dream interpretation. Cayce was able to astound people by interpreting their dreams and giving them insight into their psyche, lives and even past lives. Cayce revealed that dreams are actually journeys into the spirit world.

Edgar Cayce once said, *"Dreams, visions, impressions, to the entity in the normal sleeping state are the presentations of the experiences necessary for the development, if the entity would apply them in the physical life. These may be taken as warnings, as advice, as conditions to be met, conditions to be viewed in a way and manner as lessons, as truths, as they are presented in the various ways and manners."*

Cayce believed that our dreams serve several functions. Somatic dreams - dreams referring to the body - are extremely important to be mindful of. Very often dreams will offer solutions to health problems. For example, one man was plagued with food allergies for many years but was unable to find the source of his discomfort. Then one night he went to bed and he dreamed of a can of coffee. He quit drinking coffee and his symptoms disappeared.

Cayce also believed that deceased friends and family members do occasionally visit us in our dream state. These occurrences may offer direct communication with those people or allow us to resolve our feelings about their death. The person may also represent some aspect of themselves.

During the dreaming state of sleep, we experience the different levels of consciousness and receive input from the different realms of the spirit world. Through dreaming, we have special access to our spirit within. According to the Cayce readings, *'there is not a question we can ask which cannot be answered from the depths of our inner consciousness when the proper atunement is made.'*

A dream may be of a physical, mental, or spiritual nature and may deal with all manner of psychic manifestations. These include telepathy, clairvoyance, prophetic visions, out of body traveling, remembrance of past lives, communication with beings in other realms including deceased friends and relatives, spirit guides, angels, Christ, and even the voice of God. Dreams can also give invaluable information on the status of the body.

Cayce felt that there is no dimension of human life, whether social, financial, emotional or physical, mental or spiritual with which the dream may not on occasion deal. Dreams may encourage or reprimand, instruct or deceive, inspire or seduce, guide or confuse.

The potential for an immense array of experiences in consciousness is always there. What we actually receive depends upon our attitudes, motivations, the measure of our atunement, and the extent to which we have made applicable what was received in earlier dreams and in waking experiences.

The dream world is a strange yet fascinating place! There are several different kinds of dreams. Let us explore them in the next section.

TYPES of DREAMS

Daydreams

Studies show that we all have the tendency to daydream an average of 70-120 minutes a day. Day dreaming is classified as a level of consciousness between sleep and wakefulness. It occurs during our waking hours when we let our imagination carry us away. As our minds begin to wander and our level of awareness decreases, we lose ourselves in our imagined scenario and fantasy.

Lucid Dreams

Lucid dreams are the dreams where the dreamer is aware of dreaming. This type of dreaming is likened to out of body experiences. During lucid dreaming, the dreamer can exert some degree of control over the dream characters, narrative, and environment, basically it is the ability to consciously observe and/or control your dreams. Most dreamers wake themselves up once they realize that they are only dreaming. Other dreamers have cultivated the skill to remain in the lucid state of dreaming. They become an active participant in their own dreams, making decisions in their dreams and influencing the dream's outcome without awakening.

Nightmares

A nightmare is a disturbing dream that causes the dreamer to wake up feeling anxious and frightened. Nightmares may be a response to real life trauma and situations. This type of nightmare falls under a special category called Post-traumatic Stress Nightmare (PSN).

Nightmares may also occur because we have ignored or refused to accept a particular life situation. Research shows that most people who have regular nightmares have had a family history of psychiatric problems, bad drug experiences, people who have contemplated suicide, and/or rocky relationships.

Nightmares are an indication of a fear that needs to be acknowledged and confronted. It is a way for our subconscious to aid us in taking notice. "Pay attention!" More on nightmares can be found later in the book including steps you can take to overcome them.

Recurring Dreams

Recurring dreams repeat themselves with little variation in story or theme. These dreams may be positive, but most often they are nightmarish in content. Dreams may recur because a conflict depicted in the dream remains unresolved or ignored. Once you have found a resolution to the problem, your recurring dreams will cease.

Healing Dreams

Healing dreams serve as messages for the dreamer in regard to their health. Many dream experts believe that dreams can help us avoid potential health problems and help us to heal when we are ill. Our bodies are able to communicate to us through our dreams to "tell" us that something is not quite right with our bodies even before any physical symptoms show up. Dreams of this nature may be telling the dreamer that he/she needs to go to the dentist or doctor

Prophetic Dreams

Prophetic dreams also referred to as precognitive or psychic dreams are dreams that seemingly foretell the future. One rational theory to explain this phenomenon is that our dreaming mind is able to piece together bits of information and observation that we normally overlook or that we do not seriously consider. In other words, our unconscious mind knows what is coming before we consciously piece together the same information

Signal Dreams

Signal dreams help to solve problems or make decisions in your waking life. Signal dreams 'announce' that something in our life is, or is about to, change. There is vivid memory of these dreams upon awakening and one can't shake the feeling of trying to recieve what the message was.

Epic Dreams

Epic dreams (or Great dreams) are compelling, and so vivid that you cannot ignore them. The details of such dreams remain with you for years, as if your dreamt it last night. These dreams possess much beauty and contain many archetypal (certain kind of person or thing) symbology. When you wake up from such a dream, you feel that you have discovered something profound or amazing about yourself, or about the world. It feels like a life-changing experience.

So... what is going on in our heads when we dream?

WHY DO WE DREAM?

The brain receives stimuli from many different sources all day long. There are far too many stimuli for it to process. The mind prioritizes the stimuli and makes you aware of those that need immediate attention (the crying baby, the out-of-control car, your boss' request) so that you may act accordingly.

The stimuli that you are not consciously aware of are nevertheless noted by the brain and received automatically on a subconscious level (the drip of the bathroom water faucet, the remark by a work mate while you were on the telephone.)

Furthermore, you feel emotions all day. Some you acknowledge and act on (you say thank you and smile when you are complimented or like something). Some you repress or do not allow yourself to act on, your secret unspoken words (annoyed with your boss or partner)

Traumatic experiences occur that you face or if it too painful, you deny them happening and send them deep into your subconscious (repression.)

In addition to all these emotions and stimuli the brain must process daily, it also keeps your body functioning; it remembers names and faces; it allows you to talk, walk, chew gum, breathe; and performs numerous other activities that you take for granted.

At night, when our body must rest, the mind continues working. When are no longer called upon to send emails, work or do the grocery shopping, the brain concentrates on processing all of those subconscious stimuli and emotions (while still maintaining body temperature and breathing along with all other functioning.)

This is why we dream. Only you are not awake to receive the signals at a conscious level -- you cannot hear or see or touch (at a conscious level) while you are sleeping. The brain must resort to other means to get the signals through to your conscious mind. This is why we dream the way we do.

The mind uses everything at its disposal (which is everything it has ever been exposed to) to get the message across. Simply put, dreaming is the minds way of processing all of the stimuli and emotions it has received during the day or repressed over time, so that you may act on them.

All in all, it's a pretty neat system. But unless you are remembering and making sense of your dreams, you are missing out on countless opportunities to learn about yourself and experience life to its fullest.

Even though this has been mentioned earlier on, it bears repeating. Why should you try and remember your dreams?

WHY REMEMBER YOUR DREAMS?

Your dreaming mind has access to information that is not readily available to you when you are awake. Your dreams may reveal your secret desires and subconscious feelings.

In remembering your dreams, you will have an increased knowledge about yourself, bring about self-awareness and self-healing. Dreams are an extension of how you perceive yourself. They can be a source of inspiration, wisdom, and joy.

Dreams are always "true"—it's just the meaning is not always what we think they are. Sometimes a dream gives a warning of danger, but if you pay attention to the dream and change your ways, the danger can dissipate. And most often a dream's meaning will be metaphorical, not literal.

For example, a woman may dream that her husband is having a sexual affair, but it would be a mistake to conclude that her husband is really having an affair. The dream is simply providing the woman graphic evidence that she somehow feels betrayed by her husband. Once she acknowledges that feeling, she can then start examining her life consciously—and honestly—to find out why she feels betrayed and what she needs to do about it.

All dreams essentially tell us one important thing: "Wake up. Pay attention!" Just as you wake up from a dream to remember it, the dream itself is telling you to "wake up" to the truth that you try to hide from others—and from yourself.

Of course, there is a positive as well as a negative side to remembering and interpreting your dreams.

The negative side is that you may come across a side of yourself that you really don't like or are afraid to know about. You may discover that you are not (always) the person you act as and profess to be during the day, your masks can be revealed. You may discover that your childhood was not as pleasant as you may believe it to be. You may end up shedding light on dark places and recall secrets long repressed. This can be unnerving and life changing.

The positive side is that you go through a metamorphosis or the process of releasing, providing yourself relief from strong or repressed emotions; and become -- you. You become the "you" that you were always meant to be. You will become truer to yourself and therefore, you will find that you are happier.

Learning to recall your dreams may help you become a more assertive, creative person. In remembering your dreams, you are expressing and confronting your feelings. Remembering your dreams can help you unfold and deal with stressful aspects of your life.

But this may be easier said than done. Five minutes after the end of the dream, half the content is forgotten. After ten minutes, 90% is lost. Dreamers, who are awakened right after REM sleep, are able to recall their dreams more vividly than those who slept through the night until morning.

Recalling your dreams is vital to interpreting them.

So, how can you better remember your dreams?

HOW TO REMEMBER YOUR DREAMS

When beginning the steps towards interpreting your dreams, many people find it helpful to keep a notebook – a dream journal, if you will – right next to your bed with a pen or pencil. As soon as you are physically able, begin your journal.

Write down your dream as soon as you remember it. Write down everything you remember, even if it doesn't make sense. Most often, the parts that don't make sense or are out of place are the most valuable. Every detail, even the minutest element in your dream is important and must be considered when analysing your dreams. Look closely at the characters, animals, objects, places, emotions, and even colour and numbers that are depicted in your dreams.

Ask yourself, "What does this remind me of?" Write down the first thing that comes to your mind. This will likely be the real situation in your life that is symbolized in the dream. There is thought and thinking. Thought is intuition, the first idea that comes to mind, your Divine (Souls) voice. Thinking is ego, ideas that come to mind based on what our environments have moulded us to be and think.

Continue writing your thoughts of what it reminds you of. What did that real-life situation make you feel like? If this is the same feeling represented in your dream, you're on the right track. Often when there is more than one part to your dream (more than one story line) that usually means there are two things your subconscious is trying to tell you.

Remember that we have between four and seven dreams per night. If you wake up from a dream, write it down. Don't roll over and go back to sleep. If you don't write it down, you'll never remember it in the morning! At the very least, you can jot down the basic premise of the dream and go back in the morning to fill in the rest of the details such as feelings and other aspects.

Suggest to yourself every night as you fall asleep, "I will remember my dreams." Say this over and over. Command your sub-conscious mind. Your sub-conscious will act on this suggestion. Practice keen observation in your dreams through self-suggestion prior to sleep. When a problem confronts you, you might want to ask by prayer for guidance to be sent to you through your dreams.

Trust your instincts! If something seems important, it probably is. Try not to let your logical side take over.

So, you've got your dreams down on paper. Where do you go next? The next step is the dream interpretation.

INTERPRETING YOUR DREAMS

Interpreting your dreams can be a lot of fun. As we've said, it can also give you valuable insight. Dreams are like coded messages from your unconscious mind. When you decode them, you gain access to a wealth of intuitive wisdom.

Remember that only **you** can interpret your dreams. Many people have published "Dream Dictionaries" that describe what each part of the dream symbolizes. Actually, the same dream can have infinite meanings, depending on the person who dreamed it. The important thing is, what does it mean to **YOU**?

Interpreting dreams isn't something you can pick up and become an expert at right away. It takes time and practice. First, keep the following things in mind:

- Dreams are the reaction of the inner self to daytime activity and often show the way out of the dilemma. So, relate them to current activity, because dreams may be retrospective as well as prospective.

- Observe carefully recurrent dreams, as well as the serially progressive ones. These often illustrate progress or failure.

- Be practical in your interpretations. Always look first for a lesson. What have you refused to face or been ignoring?

- Dreams come to guide and help, not to amuse. They direct your attention to errors of omission and commission and offer encouragement for right endeavours. They also give us the opportunity to pray for others and to help them bear their burdens.

- Look for past-life experiences in your dreams. These manifest themselves not only in colour, but in the proper costume and setting of their period. They come to warn you against repeating the same old mistakes; to explain your relationship and reactions to certain people and places; to reduce your confusions; to enable you to better understand life.

- Dreams that are unchanged through the years indicate the dreamer's resistance to change.

The difficulty most people have with interpreting their own dreams is that they aren't objective enough. Their familiarity with the people and places in their dreams obscures the dreams meaning. Experts have come up with the "I AM and I NEED" formula, devised to overcome this. Here is how it works.

<u>I AM and I NEED Technique</u>

Once you have your dream written on paper, get two different coloured pens.

1. Using one colour, underline every negative word or phrase in the dream which indicates limitation, disrespect, containment, avoidance or damage.

2. Using the other colour, underline every positive word or phrase.

3. You now make two lists. List the negative words and phrases under a column titled I AM. List the positive words and phrases under a column titled I NEED. You are almost ready to interpret your dream.

Determine the subject matter of the dream. The location where the dream takes place is one of the best methods for doing this. When you have determined the subject matter take each of the phrases or words in the 'I AM' column and fit them into the following sentence…

When it comes to my (*subject matter*) I AM (*phrase or keyword*)

Change the phrase or keyword slightly to force the sentence to make sense. If you cannot determine the subject matter apply the keywords to yourself in general. This exercise tells you how you feel or react to the subject matter of the dream. When you have done this read through the 'I NEED' column to learn what you must do to correct the problem. To get the meaning put each of the phrases or keywords into the sentence...

When it comes to my (*subject matter*) I NEED (*phrase or keyword*)

Let's take an example. Using the sentence 'The dead woman lay on the cold hard slab'. The negative keywords are; dead, cold and hard. Women, in dreams, can represent emotions so in this case the sentences constructed would be...

When it comes to my *emotions* I am *dead*.

When it comes to my *emotions* I am *cold*.

When it comes to my *emotions* I am *hard*.

The meaning is obvious. With analysing just one sentence from a dream we have learned a lot about the dreamer. Using this technique, you now have all of the information you need to start interpreting your dreams. However, it takes practice to be able to apply what you have learned. Be patient with your efforts.

Not all dream interpretations will be that cut and dried, but it is a way to remain objective when you are analysing what your dreams mean and how best to put the messages they are conveying to good use in your life.

Keep in mind that <u>most</u> dreams are **<u>NOT</u>** precognitive (future vision), and once one learns the subtle differences between a precognitive dream versus a regular dream, they are easily discernible and will put your mind at ease.

The first thing everyone should consider is the typical universal symbology of the dream images. For instance, death symbolizes the end of something that's ready for change, and a new beginning. Most people start out highly resistive to changes of any sort and see any upcoming change in their life as something foreboding and scary. Death dreams are usually about change.

The symbols and what they represent is the most fascinating part of dream interpretation. There are literally hundreds of them. Here we do not address ALL of them, this would require volumes of books, however, we will touch on some of the most recurring themes in dreams as well as the symbols of those dreams and what they mean.

MOST COMMON DREAM IMAGES

One very important thing to keep in mind is to interpret symbols within the context of the dream they appear in, rather than piece by piece which would leave too much room for error. There are thousands of symbols, and it depends upon the context of one's own personal dream as to what they all mean for him or her.

A dream is much like a puzzle, and although there are several pieces that are quickly pieced together because they are so obvious, the puzzle is not complete until all the pieces are placed together bit by bit. Then you have the complete picture...until then, you'll only have disjointed images that don't add up to anything coherent, and you'll still be confused.

So please remember that and try not to piecemeal a dream...it needs to be fully interpreted or it will most likely be totally wrong.

Let's look at some of the more common dream images and what they could mean.

Teeth Falling Out

This is probably the most prevalent dream image that people report. It is disturbing to them because it affects vanity and personal appearance – but only in the dream! a dream about one's teeth falling out usually symbolizes that the dreamer is having a challenge getting their voice heard, or feelings acknowledged.

This may be referring to their conversations with a particular person such as their significant other, boss, or friend; or can be generalized for people who are shy, to include almost everyone they come in contact with.

The dreamer needs to brush up on conversational skills, believe in the value of their own opinion, and learn how to be less intimidated by aggressive people, and become more assertive and make their voice heard. Once they do that, this dream (which is a common recurring dream) should evolve & show improvement...or disappear altogether.

Another theory is that dreams about your teeth reflect your anxiety about your appearance and how others perceive you. Sadly, we live in a world where good looks are valued highly and your teeth play an important role in conveying that image. Teeth are used in the game of flirtations, whether it is a dazzling and gleaming smile or affectionate necking. These dreams may stem from a fear of your sexual impotence or the consequences of getting old. Teeth are an important feature of our attractiveness and presentation to others. Everybody worries about how they appear to others. Caring about our appearance is natural and healthy.

There are cultural interpretations of this type of dream as well. A scriptural interpretation for bad or falling teeth indicate that you are putting your faith, trust, and beliefs in what man thinks rather than in the word of God. The bible says that God speaks once, yea twice in a dream or a vision in order to hide pride from us, to keep us back from the pit, to open our ears (spiritually) and to instruct and correct us.

In the Greek culture, when you dream about loose, rotten, or missing teeth, it indicates that a family member or close friend is very sick or even near death.

According to the Chinese, there is a saying that your teeth will fall out if you are telling lies.

It has also been said that if you dream of your teeth falling out, then it symbolizes money. This is based on the old tooth fairy story. If you lose a tooth and leave it under the pillow, a tooth fairy would bring you money.

Flying

Dreams about flying usually represent freedom from the physical body, as we experience in sleep & while dreaming where we don't use our physical bodies but instead use our mental & spiritual bodies to experience our dreams. It's one of the first things people attempt to do when they gain control of their dreams and start lucid dreaming.

Everybody seems to have a natural inclination to want to fly, unless that is changed by a fear of flying due to a frightening incident in their waking lives. Flying = freedom; either a desire for freedom, an "escape" from restraints in your physical life (like a mini-vacation for the mind) or any number of possibilities.

Tie it in with the context of your dream...what were you doing in your dream besides flying? How did it make you feel? Also, the type of flying here is the person flying on their own without an airplane or any aircraft at all. That would be a different symbol dealing with spiritual awareness, among other things.

Flying dreams fall under a category of dreams where you become aware that you are dreaming, known as lucid dreaming. Many dreamers have described the ability to fly in their dreams as an exhilarating, joyful, and liberating experience.

If you are flying with ease and enjoying the scene and landscape below, then it suggests that you are on top of a situation. You have risen above something. It may also mean that you have gained a different perspective on things. Flying dreams and the ability to control your flight is representative of your own personal sense of power.

Having difficulties staying in flight indicates a lack of power in controlling your own circumstances. You may be struggling to stay aloft and stay on course. Things like power lines, trees, or mountains may further obstruct your flight. These barriers represent a particular obstacle or person who is standing in your way in your waking life. You need to identify who or what is hindering you from moving forward.

If you are feeling fear when you are flying or that you feel that you are flying too high then it suggests that you are afraid of challenges and of success.

In reality, we do not have the ability to fly. Thus such dreams may represent that which is beyond our physical limitations. In your mind, you can be anybody and do anything. Another way of interpreting flying dreams is that these dreams symbolize your strong mind and will. You feel undefeatable and nobody can tell you what you cannot do and accomplish. Undoubtedly these dreams leave you a great sense of freedom.

Being Caught In A Tornado

This symbol points to emotional turmoil, as in a "whirlwind of emotions"; and/or rapid or sudden changes in your life. It is a sign to "get a grip" on what is possibly spinning out of control & deal more effectively with your emotions. Meditation and finding some private "think time" for yourself would be a good idea.

Being Naked

Dreaming that you are completely or partially naked is very common. Nudity symbolizes a variety of things depending on your real life situation.

Becoming mortified at the realization that you are walking around naked in public is often a reflection of your vulnerability or shamefulness. You may be hiding something and are afraid that others can nevertheless see right through you. Metaphorically clothes are a means of concealment. With clothes, you can hide your identity or be someone else. But without them, everything is hanging out for all to see. You are left without any defences.

The dream may be telling you that you are trying to be something that you really are not. Or that you are fearful of being ridiculed and disgraced. If you are in a new relationship, you may have some fears or apprehension in revealing your true feelings.

Nudity also symbolizes being caught off guard.

Finding yourself naked at work or in a classroom, suggests that you are unprepared for a project at work or school. You may be uninformed in making a well-formed decision. With all eyes on you, you have this fear of having some deed brought to public attention. You fear that people will see through your true self and you will be exposed as a fraud or a phony.

Many times, when you realize that you are naked in your dream, no one else seems to notice. Everyone else in the dream is going about their business without giving a second look at your nakedness. This implies that your fears are unfounded; no one will notice except you. You may be magnifying the situation and making an issue of nothing. On the other hand, such dreams may mean your desire (or failure) to get noticed.

For a small percentage of you, dreaming that you are proud of your nakedness and show no embarrassment or shame, then it symbolizes your unrestricted freedom.

You have nothing to hide and are proud of who you are. The dream is about a new sense of honesty, openness, and a carefree nature.

Being Chased

Chase dreams often stem from feelings of anxiety in your walking life. The way we respond to anxiety and pressure in real life is typically manifested as a chase dream. Running is an instinctive response to physical threats in our environment.

Often in these dream scenarios, you are being pursued by some attacker, who wants to hurt or possibly kill you. You are running away, hiding, or trying to outwit your pursuer.

Chase dreams may represent your way of coping with fears, stress or various situations in your waking life. Instead of confronting the situation, you are running away and avoiding it. Ask yourself who is the one chasing you and you may gain some understanding and insight on the source of your fears and pressure.

The pursuer or attacker who is chasing you in your dream may also represent a part of yourself. Your own feelings of anger, jealousy, fear, and possibly love, can assume the appearance of threatening figure. You may be projecting these feelings onto the unknown chaser. Next time you have a chase dream, turn around and confront your pursuer. Ask them why they are chasing you.

One may be consumed by their own anger, jealousy, love, or self-destructive behavior. For example, you may be drinking too much or exhibiting open hostility toward others around you. You may subconsciously be threatened by these actions which have been jeopardizing your relationships and/or career. Your dreams are a way of calling attention to these self-destructive actions.

A more direct analysis of chase dreams is the fear of being attacked. Such dreams are more common among women than men, who may feel physically vulnerable in the urban environment. These dreams are inspired by fears of violence and sexual assault in which we are so over-exposed from the media. The violence that the media portrays magnifies our fears and how at risk we all are.

Falling

Falling dreams are another theme that is quite common in the world of dreams. As we said earlier, contrary to a popular myth, you will not actually die if you do not wake up before your hit the ground during a fall.

As with most common dream themes, falling is an indication of insecurities, instabilities, and anxieties. You are feeling overwhelmed and out of control in some situation in your waking life.

This may reflect the way you feel in your relationship or in your work environment. You have lost your foothold and can not hang on or keep up with the hustle and bustle of daily life. When you fall, there is nothing that you can hold on to. You more or less are forced toward this downward motion without any control. This loss of control may parallel a waking situation in your life.

Falling dreams also often reflect a sense of failure or inferiority in some circumstance or situation. It may be the fear of failing in your job/school, loss of status, or failure in love. You feel shameful and lack a sense of pride. You are unable to keep up with the status quo or that you don't measure up.

According to Freudian theory, dreams of falling indicate that you are contemplating giving into a sexual urge or impulse. You may be lacking indiscretion.

Falling dreams typically occur during the first stage of sleep. Dreams in this stage are often accompanied by muscle spasms of the arms, legs, and the whole body. These sudden contractions, also known as myclonic jerks. Sometimes when we have these falling dreams, we feel our whole-body jerk or twitch and we awaken from this jerk. It is thought that this jerking action is part of an arousal mechanism that allows the sleeper to awaken and become quickly alert and responsive to possible threats in the environment.

According to biblical interpretations, dreams about falling have a negative overtone and suggest that man is acting and walking according to his own way of thinking and not those of the Lord.

Taking An Exam or Test

To dream that you are taking an exam indicates that you are being put to the test or being scrutinized in some way. Such dreams highlight your feelings of being anxious and agitated. You may find that you cannot answer any of the questions on the test or that the test is in some foreign language.

Is time running out and you find that you can not complete the exam in the allowed time? Or are you late to the exam? Does your pencil keep breaking during the exam? Such factors contribute to you failing this test.

These dreams usually have to do with your selfesteem and confidence or your lack of. You are worried that you are not making the grade and measuring up to other people's expectations of you. You may also experience the fear of not being accepted, not being prepared, or not being good enough. You feel nervous, insecure and tend to believe the worst about yourself.

These dreams also suggest that you may feel unprepared for a challenge. Rarely, are these dreams about the content of the test, but rather the process and how you are feeling during the exam taking process. Generally, you feel distressed and frustrated. These feelings may parallel how you are feeling in a particular challenge or situation in your waking like.

Dreams of this nature are also an indication that you are being judged and this dream is a signal for you to examine an aspect of yourself that you may have been neglecting and need to pay attention to. You may harbor some guilt because of your neglect in preparation for a school exam, meeting, business project, or some challenge. Most of the time people who have such dreams are unlikely to fail a test in real life. This dream goes back to their fear and own anxiety that they may not meet other's standards of them. They are afraid to let others down.

Now let's look at some specific symbols that appear in dreams and what they might mean.

DREAM SYMBOLS

Animals

To see animals in your dream represents your own physical characteristic, primitive desires, and sexual nature, depending on the qualities of the particular animal. Animals symbolize the untamed and uncivilized aspects of who you are. Thus, to dream that you are fighting with an animal signifies a hidden part of yourself that you are trying to reject and push back into your subconscious. Refer to the specific animal in your dream.

To dream that animals can talk, represents superior knowledge. Its message is often some form of wisdom. Alternatively, a talking animal denotes your potential to be all that you can be.

To dream that you are saving the life of an animal, suggests that you are successfully acknowledging certain emotions and characteristics represented by the animal. The dream may also stem from feelings of inadequacy or being overwhelmed.

To see lab animals in your dream, suggests that an aspect of yourself is being repressed. You feel that you are not able to fully express your desires and emotions. Alternatively, it suggests that you need to experiment with your fears, choices, and beliefs. Try not to limit yourself.

People

Every person that appears in a dream is supposed to represent an aspect of ones self, and not actually be about that other person at all; rather, it is a quality or characteristic about that person that your dream is focusing on, and how it applies to YOU.

Try to think about what aspect(s) this could be. It can be something you admire and wish to emulate and incorporate into your own personality, or it could be a more negative characteristic that you may dislike intensely in your waking life, but which is telling you something about yourself and your beliefs, judgments, & attitude.

It could be a call to alter your thinking in some manner, in order to be more open-minded and accepting of this aspect in their and your own personality, because it is hampering your spiritual growth & making life harder for yourself.

The other person in your dream is always mirroring something back to you about YOURSELF. Try to discover what that something is and go from there. Once you get it through your head that the other person's appearance in your dream is NOT about them, but really about YOU, then you will get much more successful interpreting your own dreams. This takes constant reinforcing--I still find myself wanting to think it's about that other person instead of me. The only exception I know of is if the dream is precognitive.

<u>Babies or Pregnancy</u>

To dream that you are pregnant, symbolizes an aspect of yourself or some aspect of your personal life that is growing and developing. You may not be ready to talk about it or act on it. This may also represent the birth of a new idea, direction, project or goal.

To dream that you are pregnant with the baby dying inside of you suggests that a project you had put a lot of effort into is falling apart and slowly deteriorating. Nothing works out the way you want it to.

If you are pregnant and having this dream, then it represents your anxieties about the pregnancy. In the first trimester, your dreams usually consist of tiny creatures, fuzzy animals, flowers, fruit and water.

In the second trimester, your dreams will reflect your anxiety about being a good mother and concerns about possible complications with the birth. Dreams of giving birth to a non-human baby are also common during this period of the pregnancy. Finally, in the third trimester, you will tend to dream about your own mother.

For a man to dream that he got a girl pregnant, forewarns that his indiscriminate sexual activities may come back to haunt him

To see a baby in your dream signifies innocence, warmth and new beginnings. Babies may symbolize something in your own inner nature which is pure, vulnerable, and/or uncorrupted. Babies may represent an aspect of yourself that is vulnerable and helpless. If you dream that you forgot you had a baby, then it suggests that you are trying hide your own vulnerabilities; You do not want to let others know of your weaknesses.

If you dream that you are on your way to the hospital to have a baby, then it signifies your issues of dependency and your desire to be completely care for. Perhaps you are trying to get out of some responsibility. If you are pregnant, then a more direct interpretation may simply mean that you are experiencing some anxieties of making it to the hospital when the time comes.

To dream of a crying baby, is indicative of a part of yourself that is deprived of attention and needs some nurturing. Alternatively, it represents your unfulfilled goals and a sense of lacking in your life.

To dream about a starving baby, represents your dependence on others. You are experiencing some deficiency in your life that needs immediate attention and gratification.

To dream of an extremely small baby, symbolizes your helplessness and your fears of letting others become aware of your vulnerabilities and incompetence. You may be afraid to ask for help and as a result tend to take matters into your own hands.

To see a dead baby in your dream, symbolizes the ending of something that is part of you.

To dream that you are dipping a baby in and out of water signifies regression. You are regressing to a time where you had no worries and responsibilities.

Alternatively, it is reminiscing of when the baby is in the foetus and in its comfort zone. In fact, some expectant mothers even give birth in a pool, because the environment in the water mimics the environment in the uterus. It is less traumatic for the baby as it emerges into the world. So perhaps the dream is your search for your own comfort zone.

Sex

To dream about sex, refers to the psychological completion and the integration of contrasting aspects of the Self. You need to be more receptive and incorporate aspects of your dream sex partner into your own character. Alternatively, and a more direct interpretation of the dream, may be your libido's way of telling you that it's been too long since you have had sex. It may indicate repressed sexual desires and your needs for physical and emotional love.

To dream about sex with someone other than your spouse or significant other, suggests dissatisfaction with the physical side of your relationship. On the other hand, it may be harmless fantasy. In such situations, you may find that you are less inhibited sexually and you can even bring that sense of adventure to your existing relationship.

To dream that you are having sex with an ex or someone who is not your current mate, denotes your reservations about embarking in a new relationship or situation. You may feel nervous about exposing yourself or currently feel a resurgence of those old emotions and feelings that you felt back when you and your ex were together.

Believe it or not, it is not uncommon for people approaching their wedding to experience especially erotic adventures with partners other than their intended spouses. This may be due to the intensity of your sexual passion with your fiancé. It also relates to the new roles that you will be taking on and the uncertainty that that may bring.

If you are heterosexual and you dream that you are having sex with someone of the same sex, signifies not necessarily homosexual desire, but an expression of greater self love and acceptance. You need to be in better touch of your feminine or masculine side.

To dream that you are the opposite sex, suggests that you exhibit or need to incorporate those qualities of the opposite sex. Ask yourself, how do you feel being a man or a woman? In what ways can you incorporate those feelings into your waking life?

Snakes

Snakes are complicated dream symbols and have both positive and negative meanings.

To see a snake or be bitten by one in your dream signifies hidden fears and worries that are threatening you. Your dream may be alerting you to something in your waking life that you are not aware of or that has not yet surfaced. The snake may also be seen as phallic and thus symbolize dangerous and forbidden sexuality. The snake may also refer to a person around you who is callous, ruthless, and can't be trusted. As a positive symbol, snakes represent transformation, knowledge and wisdom. It is indicative of self-renewal and positive changes.

Snakes can also represent primal energy, temptation and evil. These could be the thoughts and feelings you may be trying to suppress. In constantly suppressing your feelings, over time it will overflow to the point where you are forced to confront them.

Fire

Depending on the context of your dream, to see fire in your dream can symbolizes destruction, passion, desire, illumination, transformation, enlightenment, or anger. It may suggest that something old is passing and something new is entering your life. Your thoughts and views are changing. In particular, if the fire is under control or contained in one area, it is a metaphor of your own internal fire and inner transformation. It also represents your drive and motivation.

To dream of that you are being burned by fire, indicates that your temper is getting out of control. Some issue or situation is burning you up inside.

To dream that a house is on fire indicates that you need to undergo some transformation. If you have recurring dreams of your family house on fire, then it suggests that you are still not ready for the change or that you are fighting against the change. Alternatively, it highlights passion and the love of those around you.

To dream that you put out a fire signifies that you will overcome your obstacles in your life through much work and effort.

Trains

To see a train in your dream represents conformity and go along with what everyone else is doing. You have the need to do things in an orderly and sequential manner. In particular, if you see a freight train, then it refers to the burdens and problems that you are hauling around.

To dream that you are on a train, is symbolic of your life's journey and suggests that you are on the right track in life and headed for the right direction. Alternatively, you have a tendency to worry needlessly over a situation that will prove to work out in the end.

To see or dream that you are in a train wreck, suggests chaos. The path towards achieving your goals is not going according to the way you planned it out. Or you may be lacking self-confidence and having doubt in your ability to reach your goals.

To dream that you are the engineer signifies that you are in complete control of a particular situation in your waking life.

To dream that you miss a train denotes missed opportunities or nearly escaping your death.

Driving

To dream that you are driving a vehicle signifies your life's journey and your path in life. The dream is telling of how you are moving and navigating through life.

If you are driving and cannot see the road ahead of you, then it indicates that you do not know where you are headed in life and what you really want to do with yourself. You are lacking direction and goals. If you are driving on a curvy road, then it indicates that you are having difficulties in achieving your goals and the changes associated with it.

To dream that someone else is driving you represents your dependence on the driver. You are not in control of your life and following the goals of others instead of your own. If you are driving from the passenger side of a car, then it suggests that you are trying to gain control of the path that your life is taking. You are beginning to make your own decisions.

To dream that you are driving a cab or bus symbolizes menial labor with little opportunities for advancement.

To dream that you are driving a car in reverse suggests that you are experiencing major setbacks in your goals. In particular, if you drive in reverse into a pool of water, then it means that you emotions are literally holding you back.

To dream that you are driving drunk indicates that your life is out of control. Some relationship or somebody is dominating you.

To dream that you drive off a mountain road suggests that the higher you climb in life, the harder it is to stay at the top. You feel that your advanced position is a precarious one. It takes hard work to remain at the top. You may also feel that you are not able to measure up to the expectations of others.

Seeing a wreck in your dream represents obstacles and barriers toward your goals. You feel that you are being held back or that you are not making any progress.

The car or vehicle itself is supposed to symbolize you in your waking life, in your physical body. Your physical body is used by the soul pretty much like we use a car...it's driven for awhile and we give it gas/nourishment & repairs as needed until it stops running, and then we go back home.

Pay attention to your car, which symbolizes your physical body. Are you behind the wheel, or is someone else in control? You want to be in charge of your life, naturally. What is the colour & condition of this vehicle? Do you seem to be driving it the right way, on a safe road in good condition, or is the road rocky, winding, or suddenly ends at a cliff? That would signal you need redirection.

The bigger the vehicle, the more energy you may be successfully using for your daily lessons, depending on the context of your dream. Note all clues as to how you are faring and make adjustments accordingly.

Ex-Partners

To dream about your ex-boyfriend/girlfriend or ex-husband/wife or that you and your ex got back together again, suggests that something or someone in your current life that is bringing out similar feelings you felt during the relationship with your ex.

The dream may be a way of alerting you to the same or similar behaviour in a current relationship. What you learn from that previous relationship may need to be applied to the present one so that you do no repeat the same mistake. Alternatively, past lovers often highlight the positive experiences you had with that person.

To see your ex-husband/wife in your dream indicates that you are finding yourself in a situation that you do not want to be in. It suggests that you are experiencing a similar relationship or situation which makes you feel unhappy and uncomfortable.

To see your mate's ex in your dream suggests that you may be comparing yourself to the ex. The dream is trying to tell you not to make the same relationship mistakes that ended that relationship.

Alternatively, seeing your ex in your dream also signifies aspects of yourself that you have crossed out or neglected

To see an old ex-boyfriend or girlfriend from childhood in your dream refers to a freer, less encumbered relationship. The dream serves to bring you back to a time where the responsibilities of adulthood (or marriage) didn't interfere with the spontaneity of romance. You need to recapture the excitement, freedom, and vitality of youth that is lacking in your present relationship.

To dream that your ex-boyfriend or girlfriend is giving you advice about your current relationship suggests that your unconscious is telling you not to repeat the same mistakes that you had made with this ex.

To dream that you are being massaged by your ex suggests that you need to let go of some of that defensiveness that you have been putting forth. You may have been putting up a wall or armor around you. You need to learn to trust people again.

To dream that you ex gives you a stuffed animal suggests that you are seeking for reassuring and nurturing aspects of a relationship. This is not to imply that you want your ex back. Alternatively, the dream could represent some immature relationship which may (or may not) describe the relationship you had with your ex.

To dream that you see your ex dressed in a suit at a hospital suggests that you have come to terms with that relationship and have completed the healing process.

Cheating

To dream that you are cheating on your spouse, mate, fiancé, or significant other suggests feelings of self-guilt and self-betrayal. You may have compromised your beliefs or integrity and/or are wasting your energy and time on fruitless endeavors.

Alternatively, it reflects the intensity of your sexual passion and exploring areas of your sexuality. It is actually a reaffirmation of your commitment. Furthermore, it is not uncommon for people approaching a wedding to have dreams about erotic experiences with partners other than their intended spouses. Most likely, such dreams represent the newness of your sexual passion. It may also signify anxieties of changing your identity - that of a spouse.

To dream that your mate, spouse, or significant other is cheating on you indicates your fears of being abandoned.

You may feel a lack of attention in the relationship. Alternatively, you may feel that you are not measuring up to the expectations of others. This notion may stem from issues of trust or self-esteem. The dream could also indicate that you are unconsciously picking up hints and cues that your significant other is not being completely truth or is not fully committed in the relationship.

To dream that you are cheating at a game, suggests that you are not being honest with yourself.

School

This type of dream relates to your current "lesson in life," and if you learn how to interpret it, you'll find out how you are progressing. Think of it as taking a test and getting graded on it!

Our "true selves" are our souls, and not our physical bodies. You are a spirit/soul having a physical dream, not the other way around. Ever feel like your life is like a play, and you are acting out some role that you don't even understand, even surprising yourself with your actions sometimes? Bingo!

When we sleep, that proverbial "Veil of Forgetfulness" that prevents us from "cheating on the test" is lifted, and we are shown what type of progress we are making or not making and given guidance on what to do next.

We always have free will in our waking physical lives, though, and if we stubbornly refuse to finish our tests, then we have that right--but we are doomed to repeat it until we pass it; and each time we turn away from it, the next time it will be more unpleasant until finally we are forced to acknowledge it's importance for our growth.

The things we consider vitally important in our waking physical lives are not nearly as important as the TRUE reason we are here, which is to overcome our shortcomings so that we may get closer to our

Source/God/Higher Power. Don't avoid learning the lesson or you will find yourself repeating the same tasks over and over again never making any progress.

A House

Dreams about a house symbolize a larger aspect of your Self, and the aspects of Self which make the whole. Each room is said to symbolize a different aspect of your Self; for example:

An <u>ATTIC</u> symbolizes your Higher Self, and your spiritual development & progress. Look at other symbols in the attic of your dream and try to evaluate what they mean. Also pay attention to the feeling you experience in your dream...is it pensive, enlightening or what, exactly? All these things are clues for you.

A <u>BATHROOM</u> would symbolize the need for cleansing/purging/elimination of something in your life that isn't quite working or that has served its purpose and now it's time to move on.

A <u>KITCHEN</u> would symbolize the need or act of supplying nourishment or food for the body/mind/soul...whatever is currently "cooking" or developing in your life. If the food is plentiful, you have what you need. If the cupboard is bare, time to go shopping for new nourishment, and you need to figure out what is needed for that "shopping list."

A <u>DINING ROOM</u> is similar to the kitchen but has more to do with immediate needs for supplying & utilizing nourishment, and less with the preparation or taking stock of those needs.

THE <u>MAIN ROOM</u> or <u>LIVING ROOM</u> symbolizes your daily interactions with others, and often you will have other people appearing in your dreams in this room. Remember, they represent aspects of yourself, and not themselves. (See PEOPLE, above)

BEDROOMS symbolize the unconscious mind aspect of your self, rest, dreams, sometimes sexuality issues in your life.

THE UPSTAIRS symbolizes your spiritual awareness aspect of self, or the Higher Self that holds all the keys or knowledge to this life's role you are acting out, and always has your higher good looked after, no matter how it might seem otherwise.

THE DOWNSTAIRS/BASEMENT symbolizes your subconscious mind aspect of self, which deals with habits, old coping skills, automation, ego. That's usually the part of ourselves that makes us feel "torn" between knowing we should do one thing, and inexplicably ending up doing the opposite. Old belief patterns & fears have to be corrected, if that is the case. Tackle & overcome it, and you will feel much more peaceful about your life.

THE GROUND FLOOR of a house represents your daily agenda; what's currently going on in your life.

REVISITING OLD HOUSES FROM CHILDHOOD OR EARLIER TIMES: This points to issues that probably are resurfacing in your current life, and need to be looked at, analyzed, and healed so you can move forward and not look back. If you find yourself repeating the same old tired mistakes, or dealing with the same old tired fears, chances are you will have this dream.

A <u>HALLWAY</u> symbolizes that you have reached an area that is necessary to journey through in order to get to the other side, and it may be a narrow path that has to be traversed with care and awareness. If you have that "closed in, claustrophobic feeling" then you need to expand your awareness/open your mind to more possibilities for completing this phase of your journey.

A PORCH symbolizes perhaps a metaphor of being undecided, such as the saying, "I'm still on the porch on that decision." It could be symbolic of being contemplative, or uncommitted or withdrawn. It could be something entirely different such as being on the threshold of a new sense or an extension of self. It depends on the entire context of the dream. Is it the back or front porch? Is it screened-in or open, messy or neat, sparse or furnished? All these details add to the overall symbolism.

<u>Colours</u>

Experts believe that almost everyone dreams in colour. If a major portion of your dream reflects a consistent colour theme, this could have some type of meaning in interpreting that dream. Below are the major colours and what they could mean.

Black

Black symbolizes the unknown, unconscious, danger, mystery, darkness, death, mourning, hate or malice.

If the feeling in the dream is one of joy, blackness could imply hidden spirituality and divine qualities.

To dream in black and white, suggests that you need to be more objective in formulating your decisions. You may be a little too unyielding in your thought process and thus need to find some sort of balance between two opposing views. Consider the views and opinions of others. Alternatively, black and white dreams are signs of depression or sadness. You may feel that there is not enough excitement in your life

Blue

Blue represents truth, wisdom, heaven, eternity, devotion, tranquillity, loyalty and openness. The presence of this colour in your dream, may symbolize your spiritual guide and your optimism of the future. You have clarity of mind.

Depending on the context of your dream, the colour blue may also be a metaphor of "being blue" and feeling sad

Brown

Brown denotes worldliness, practicality, domestic and physical comfort, conservatism, and a materialistic character. Brown also represents the ground and earth

Gold

The golden colour reflects your spiritual rewards, richness, refinement and enhancement of your surroundings.

Green

Green signifies a positive change, good health, growth, healing, hope, vigor, vitality, peace, and serenity. Green is also symbolic of your strive to gain recognition and establish your independence. Money, wealth and jealousy are often associated with this colour.

Dark green indicates materialism, cheating, deceit, and/or difficulties with sharing. You need to balance between your masculine and feminine attributes.

Grey

Grey indicates fear, fright, depression, ill health, ambivalence and confusion. You may feel emotionally distant or detached.

Orange

Orange denotes friendliness, courtesy, lively, sociability, and an out-going nature. You may want to expand your horizons and look into new interests.

Pink

Pink represents love, joy, sweetness, happiness, affection, kindness. Being in love or healing through love is also implied with this colour.

Purple

Purple is indicative of devotion, healing abilities, loving, kindness, and compassion. It is also the colour of royalty, high rank, and dignity.

Red

Red is an indication of raw energy, force, vigour, intense passion, aggression, power, courage and passion. The colour red has deep emotional and spiritual connotations.

Red is also the colour of danger, shame, sexual impulses and urges. Perhaps you need to stop and think about your actions.

White

White represents purity, perfection, peace, innocence, dignity, cleanliness, awareness, and new beginnings. You may be experiencing a reawakening or have a fresh outlook on life. However, in Eastern cultures, white is associated with death and mourning

Yellow

The colour yellow has both positive and negative connotations. If the dream is a pleasant one, then the colour yellow is symbolic of intellect, energy, agility, happiness, harmony, and wisdom.

On the other hand, if the dream is an unpleasant one, then the colour represents cowardice and sickness. You may have a fear or an inability to make a decision or take action. As a result, you are experiencing many setbacks

Death

To dream about the death of a loved one, suggests that you are lacking a certain aspect or quality that the loved one embodies. Ask yourself what makes this person special or what do you like about him. It is that very quality that you are lacking in your own relationship or circumstances. Alternatively, it indicates that whatever that person represents has no part in your own life.

To dream that you die in your dream, symbolizes inner changes, transformation, self-discovery and positive development that is happening within you or in your life.

Although such dreams may bring about feelings of fear and anxiety, it is no cause for alarm and is often considered a positive symbol. Dreams of experiencing your own death usually mean that big changes are ahead for you. They mean you are moving onto new beginnings and leaving the past behind.

These changes do not necessarily imply a negative turn of events. Metaphorically, dying can be seen as an end or a termination to your old ways and habits. So, dying does not always mean a physical death, but an ending of something.

On a negative note, to dream that you die may represent involvement in deeply painful relationships or unhealthy, destructive behaviours. You may be feeling depressed or feel strangled by a situation or person in your waking life. Perhaps your mind is preoccupied with someone who is terminally ill or dying. Alternatively, you may be trying to get out of some obligation, responsibility or other situation.

To see someone dying in your dream signifies that your feelings for that person are dead or that a significant change/loss is occurring in your relationship with that person. Alternatively, you may want to repress that aspect of yourself that is represented by the dying person.

Love/Lust

To dream of love of being in love suggests intense feelings carried over from a waking relationship. It implies happiness and contentment with what you have and where you are in life. On the other hand, you may not be getting enough love in your daily life. We naturally long for the sense to belong and to be accepted.

To see a couple in love or expressing love to each other, indicates much success ahead for you.

To dream that your friend is in love with you may be one of wish fulfillment. Perhaps you have developed have developed feelings for your best friend and are wondering how he or she feels. You are so preoccupied with these thoughts that it is evitable that it finds its way into your dreaming mind.

On the other hand, the dream may also suggest that you have accepted certain qualities of your best friend and incorporated into your own character.

To dream that you are making love in public or in different places, relates to some overt sexual issue or need. Your dream may be telling you that you need to express yourself more openly. Alternatively, it represents your perceptions about your own sexuality in the context of politic and social norms. You may be questioning your feelings about sex, marriage, love, and gender roles.

To dream of lust, suggests that you are lacking or feeling unfulfilled in some aspect of your life. Alternatively, you need to exercise some self-control.

Aliens

To dream that you are an alien, symbolizes the undiscovered part of yourself. Your manifestation as an alien may be your way of 'escaping' from reality. Dreams of this nature also symbolize your outlandish ideas and your wild imagination.

To dream that you are being abducted by aliens indicates your fears of your changing surroundings or your fear of losing your home and family. You feel that your space and/or privacy is being invaded.

To see aliens in your dream signifies that you are having difficulties adapting and adjusting to your new surroundings. You are feeling "alienated" and invaded. On a psychological level, seeing aliens may represent an encounter with an unfamiliar or neglected aspect of your own self.

Angels

To see angels in your dream signifies an unusual disturbance in your soul. Angels symbolize goodness, purity, and protection and comfort and consolation. Pay careful attention to the message that the angels are trying to convey. These messages serve as a guide toward greater fulfillment and happiness. Angels may appear in your dream as a result of your wicked and mean-hearted activities.

To see an angel holding a scroll in your dream indicates a highly spiritual dream. Your future and goals are clearer to you in dreams of this type. The message on the scroll is particularly significant.

Children

To see children in your dream signifies your own childlike qualities or a retreat to a childlike state. It is an extension of your inner child during a time of innocence, purity, simplicity, and a carefree attitude. You may be longing for the past and the chance to satisfy repressed desires and unfulfilled hopes. Take some time off and cater to the inner child within. Perhaps there is something that you need to see grow and nurtured.

To dream that your own grown children are still very young indicates that you still see them as young and dependent. You want to feel needed and significant.

To dream that you are watching children, but they do not know you are there is a metaphor for some hidden knowledge or some latent talent which you have failed to recognize.

To save a child signifies your attempts to save a part of yourself from being destroyed.

Dead People

To see the dead in your dream forewarns that you are being influenced by negative people and are hanging around the wrong crowd. You may suffer material loss. This dream may also be a way for you to resolve your feelings with those who have passed on.

To see and talk with your dead father in your dream signifies that you are about to enter into an unlucky transaction or rotten deal. Thoroughly think through your decisions before entering into them.

To see your dead mother in your dream signifies your wretched and mean-hearted nature towards others around you.

Seeing your dead parents in your dreams may mean your fears of losing them or your way of coping with the loss. You may want that last opportunity to say your final good-byes to them.

To see your dead sibling, relative, or friend in your dream foretells that you will soon be called on for aid and assistance. It may also mean that you miss them and are trying to relive your old experiences you had with them. In trying to keep up with the pace of your daily waking life, you dream may serve as your only outlet in coping and coming to terms with the loss of a loved one.

Do not fear conversation with the so-called "dead" in dreams. If the communication is one-sided, it denotes telepathy. If both participate, it may be an actual encounter of bodiless consciousness.

Accidents

To dream that you are in an accident signifies pent up guilt and you are sub-consciously punishing yourself over it.

To dream of a car accident symbolizes your emotional state. You may be harbouring deep anxieties and fears. Are you "driving" yourself too hard? This dream may tell you to slow down before you hit disaster. You need to rethink or replan your course of actions and set yourself on a better path.

To dream that a loved one dies in an accident indicates that something in your own Self that is no longer functional and is "dead". It is also symbolic of your own relationship with that person. Perhaps you need to let go of this relationship.

Accident dreams may also represent your straightforward fears of being an actual, physical accident. You may be simply nervous about getting behind the wheel. This dream may be a clear warning to cautious of approaching vehicles.

This is only a general partial list – of course. Every single detail in your dream could have some hidden meaning. There are a lot of places online to find information about the specific details of your dreams and what they might mean.

You need to discover the link between all these images and what they might mean. This process is a bit like those "connect the dots" puzzles that reveal a hidden picture.

Psychologically, you simply need to understand what this net of associations from the dream is telling you specifically, at this precise time of your life, about your current problems and conflicts.

Quite often, these associations are purely emotional; that is, you can take a particularly graphic dream image, examine your emotional reactions to it, look back into your past for times when you felt the same emotions, and then ask yourself in what way those situations from the past have any bearing on what is happening in your life now

Repetitive dreams indicate that you are continuing to miss the point about the meaning of the dream. If you don't "wake up" to the unconscious meaning of the dream but instead persist in seeing it through your own wish-fulfilment needs, you will remain stuck in your own self-deception.

Almost everyone has experienced a nightmare at one point or time in their life.

NIGHTMARES

Children, especially, are prone to nightmares. Nightmares are common in children, typically beginning at around age 3 and occurring up to age 7-8.

People with anxiety disorder might also experience what experts term "night terrors". These are actually panic attacks that occur in sleep.

It is especially difficult to remember these types of dreams since they conjure up terrifying images that we would just as soon forget.

In poetic myth, the Nightmare is actually a "small nettlesome mare, not more than thirteen hands high, of the breed familiar with the Elgin marbles: cream-coloured, cleanlimbed, with a long head, bluish eye, flowing mane and tail." Her nests, called mares' nests, "when one comes across them in dreams, lodged in rock-clefs or the branches of enormous hollow yews, are built of carefully chosen twigs lined with white horse-hair and the plumage of prophetic birds and littered with the jaw-bones and entrails of poets."

Thus, in a pagan world of myth and blood sacrifice, the Nightmare was a cruel, fearful creature. Our modern word nightmare derives from the Middle English nihtmare (from niht, night, and mare, demon), an evil spirit believed to haunt and suffocate sleeping people. And so, in today's world, when we speak of a nightmare we mean a frightening dream accompanied by a sensation of oppression and helplessness.

The blood-thirsty aspect of the mythic Nightmare, however, can give a good clue about nightmares in general, for in psychodynamic terms nightmares are graphic depictions of raw, primitive emotions such as aggression and rage that have not been incorporated into the conscious psyche. Thus we tend to encounter these "ugly" aspects of our unconscious lives as terrifying dream images in whose presence we feel completely helpless.

Nightmares are quite common in childhood because this is a time of our emotional development when we all have to come to terms with, well, raw, primitive emotions such as aggression and rage.

Traumatic nightmares can also occur as one of the many symptoms of posttraumatic stress disorder (PTSD). Repetitive, intrusive nightmares following a trauma often contain symbolic themes that mirror the original trauma and relate to threat to life, threat of abandonment or death, or loss of identity.

Therefore, traumatic nightmares need to be treated differently than other dreams. It's not enough just to "know" intellectually the psychological reasons why you have these nightmares. An event is traumatic because it disrupts your previously secure—and illusory—sense of "self." And so, to heal from a trauma, you must take the initiative to make conscious changes in your life to accommodate the traumatic shattering of your illusions about life and identity.

Some believe that nightmares have a physiological nature as well. Edgar Cayce believed that Nightmares, which bring with them an inability to move or cry out, usually indicate the wrong diet. To end the nightmarish dreams change your diet.

We found a technique online that can help people who suffer from recurrent nightmares. It is not meant to be a cure-all. It is just a suggested treatment to deal with frightening nightmares. The idea is to use this therapy every night until the nightmare has been resolved. It is called Imagery Rehearsal Therapy.

Here are the steps of Imagery Rehearsal Therapy:

1. Write out the text of the nightmare. Tell the story, no matter how frightening, in as much detail as you can remember.

2.	Create a new ending for the nightmare story and write it out. Be careful, however, to make the new ending peaceful. Remember that the nightmare is grounded in emotions such as raw anger that have been provoked by a trauma. The point of a new ending is to "tame" the emotions, not merely vent them in violence and revenge.

3.	Rehearse the new version of the story in your imagination each night just before going to sleep. Do this as close as possible to your falling asleep without any other activity between the rehearsal and sleep.

4.	Perform a relaxation exercise. Do this immediately after the rehearsal, as a way to fall asleep peacefully. You may use any technique with which you are familiar. This could be meditation, yoga, or breathing exercises.

The "cousin" of nightmares is disturbing dreams with unpleasant images.

DISTURBING DREAMS

Disturbing dreams aren't quite nightmares. They may cause you to wonder what exactly your sub-conscious is trying to tell you.

First, the dreams could be unconscious advice. Maybe in some way you are betraying yourself, forgetting something, or not fulfilling a potential. For example, persons on the edge of a midlife career change may have dreams about being in school and searching for a missing classroom, or they may find themselves in a class about to take a final exam while realizing that they completely forgot to attend the class all year. Thus the feeling of panic in the dream points to the real feeling of panic in their current life about the failure of their present career.

Second, the dreams could be an admonition, based in guilt. Imagine, for example, that you are embezzling the bank for which you work. Then you start having dreams about burglars breaking into your home.

Well, the dreams are simply a depiction of something happening to you that is similar to the hurt or moral injury you are inflicting on someone else. This same dynamic often occurs in children's nightmares: in waking life, children often experience angry feelings toward their parents and yet lack the cognitive capacity to express these feelings openly; so, in unconscious guilt, the anger becomes turned against themselves as threatening nightmare images.

Third, the dreams could be hints of a repressed trauma. As I say above, nightmares often accompany the emotional pain of a traumatic event experienced in adulthood. But if a trauma in childhood is repressed, dreams reflecting the emotional intensity of the trauma can persist throughout life—as a repetition compulsion—until the trauma is eventually brought to conscious awareness and healed.

Finally, the dreams could be psychic premonitions. This is a rare phenomenon, but it does happen to some persons.

The best advice we've found about disturbing dreams is to just ignore them. You can try to analyse the images you find, but that is most likely not going to give you the answers you need.

CONCLUSION

Dream analysis and interpretation isn't the mystical science that it seems to be. It's simply remembering your dreams and then figuring out what your sub-conscious is trying to tell you about your life and anything that might be happening in your life.

You should keep in mind that dream analysis is simply an interpretation of your dreams, not a definitive answer for all that "ails" you, so to speak.

If you are having some major life problems, you can still, however, pay close attention to your dreams and we suggest you seek the assistance of a trained professional.

Your dreams are unique to you. They can represent all that is good in you and all that you need to improve upon. When you better understand your dreams, you can better understand yourself.

Remember:

"The importance of the unconscious mind, with respect to dream interpretation *and his primary theory is that the*

unconscious mind governs behaviour to a greater degree than people suspect, and the goal of psychoanalysis is to make the unconscious conscious." - Sigmund Freud

"A dream may be of a physical, mental, or spiritual nature and may deal with all manner of psychic manifestations. These include telepathy, clairvoyance, prophetic visions, out of body traveling, remembrance of past lives, communication with beings in other realms including deceased friends and relatives, spirit guides, angels, Christ, and even the voice of God. Dreams can also give invaluable information on the status of the body."
– Edgar Cayce

We wish you a pleasant slumber and ease in interpreting your guidance!

To Download your FREE accompanying A-Z Dictionary of Dream Interpretations go to:

www.perpelflame.com

About the Author

Termina listed as a global Self-Help expert and Author also known as 'The Happy Magnet' has the uncanny ability to tilt the odds so the best will happen resides with her family in Australia and believes in navigating the changing world of experiences.

As an Expansion Mentor and with a corporate background in personal development, design and business, Termina holds a range of qualifications including Transformational Leadership, Public Speaking and Medicine. Also, an exponent of Feng Shui, Termina uses her knowledge of Energy and Quantum physics to support individuals and organizations by increasing their success in financial situations, relationships, health or inspiration. Termina loves to use her imagination and has gained the title 'Master of Imagination', she has used her skills to work on many residential and commercial projects, including an open design radio station, Fox Studios and a variety of set designs, where her own artwork was exhibited for TV and film.

Termina holds the knowledge of communication in high acclaim in particular non-verbal language as this has been an exceptional skill in moving her towards her chosen goals. Termina has worked with many great minds including Bob Proctor and Peggy McColl; and adds that seeking knowledge, self-improvement and possibilities through mentors and books is the greatest gift to ourselves.

Festival of the Imagination is one of many non-fiction books by Termina. Termina calls herself a student of self-actualization. It was through her studies and introspection practices that she was able to tap into her unique soul signature and states that she is guided by source. *"At all times we carry with us all the answers. There is nothing in the physical world that will truly give us the ultimate answer; our unique soul print and purpose in life; and it is because of this only ourself has the true answers for what makes us happy or why we are here. We only require external tools, or mentors to get us started and guide us in a direction towards connecting with our soul's voice. With the right tools and mentors, we are on our way to unleashing our true, powerful self."*

Termina credits communication and self-actualization practices for her success and harmony in her life. Another one she credits is Feng Shui as a guide to alignment for choices. *"It was through my studies and practice of Feng shui that I discovered the importance this ancient art plays in our life. 33% of our experiences are created through our physical visualization board, our environment. When we apply the principles of Feng Shui our lives become the choices we desire, we are in control of our own experiences at all times and good fortune is attainable. Through Feng Shui I have seen improvements and successes in my own life along with the many others who have appointed my services."*

For more information about this author
And other books:
www.terminaashton.com
www.terminafengshui.com
www.perpelflame.com
www.thehappymagnet.com

www.ingramcontent.com/pod-product-compliance
Lightning Source LLC
Chambersburg PA
CBHW050441010526
44118CB00013B/1633